SMELLY LOCKER

JUST PLAIN
LOST

With love to my sons,
Andrew, Nathan, and David,
and to my daughter, Simone,
even though I promised not to
mention her in this dedication
—A. K.

To Mr. Reeves,
I had a hall pass—
but I lost it.
—D. C.

ISBN 978-0-545-51046-2

Text copyright © 2008 by Alan Katz.
Illustrations copyright © 2008 by David Catrow.
All rights reserved. Published by Scholastic Inc.,
557 Broadway, New York, NY 10012,
by arrangement with Margaret K. McElderry Books, an
imprint of Simon & Schuster Children's Publishing Division.
SCHOLASTIC and associated logos are trademarks
and/or registered trademarks of Scholastic Inc.

12 11 10 9 8 7 6 5 4 3 2 1   12 13 14 15 16 17/0

Printed in the U.S.A.   08

This edition first printing, September 2012

Book design by Sonia Chaghatzbanian
The text for this book is set in Kosmik.
The illustrations for this book are rendered
in watercolors, colored pencil, and ink.

SMELLY LOCKER

silly dilly school songs

by **alan katz**

illustrated by **david catrow**

SCHOLASTIC INC.

Smelly Locker!

(To the tune of "Frère Jacques")

Smelly locker!
Smelly locker!
Poor hygiene!
Foul and mean!
Meant to do it sooner.
Is this a glove or tuna?
Time to clean!
Time to clean!

Smelly locker!
Smelly locker!
Never seen
meat so green!
Stand back—its aroma
could put you in a coma!
Time to clean!
Time to clean!

Smelly locker!
Smelly locker!
Real bad scene!
Hurts my spleen!
Shoulda got permission
to put my dead pet fish in.
Time to clean!
Time to clean!

Smelly locker!
Smelly locker!
See my clothes
decompose!
Though I'm filled with sorrow,
school is closed tomorrow.
I suppose
they'll bulldoze!

Heavy Backpack!

(To the tune of "Oh! Susanna")

Oh, I just packed my new backpack
'cause the school year has begun.
Now I heard my poor old back crack
'cause the darn thing weighs a ton!

It contains a four-inch binder,
books and crayons and my lunch.
I'm now a money finder
'cause I'm walking with a hunch.

Heavy backpack!
So many pounds, I fear
if I look up, I'm gonna
topple over on my rear!

Some kids have backpacks set on wheels;
to roll them is the plan.
I put mine on and drag my heels.
Please call a moving van!

Heavy backpack!
Just lifting it I dread.
It would be easier to carry
the school home instead!

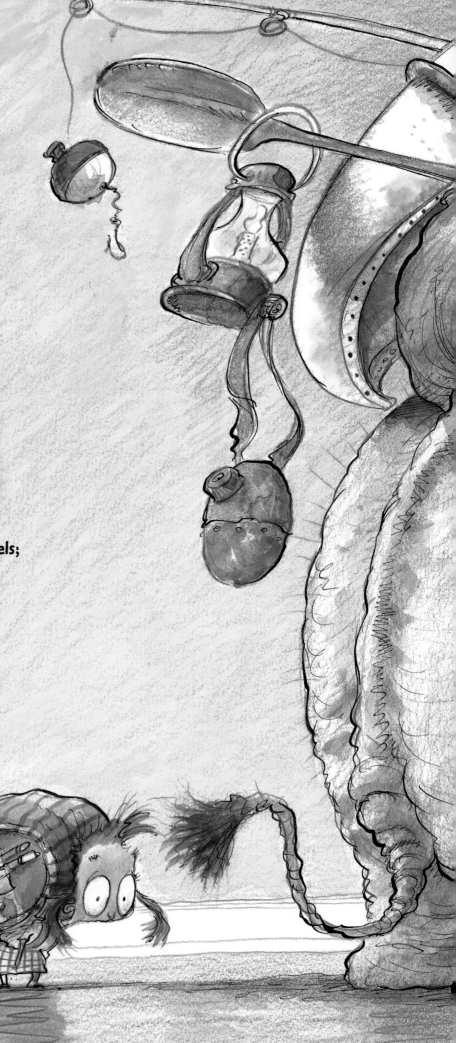

Stressed
About the Test!

(To the tune of "Miss Mary Mack")

I'm very stressed,
stressed, stressed!
Just had a test,
test, test.
I didn't study,
study, study.
And so I guessed,
guessed, guessed.
Multiple choice,
choice, choice.
Sat next to Joyce,
Joyce, Joyce.
She whispered, but,
but, but
couldn't hear her voice,
voice, voice!

So I guessed A,
A, A.
Then C,
B, C,
C, B.
For the next three,
three, three,
tried A, and B,
then C!
This guessing spree,
spree, spree
of A, B, C,
C, C,
I'd say it failed,
failed, failed.

Because you see,
see, see,
the teacher, she,
she, she
came up to me,
me, me
and said, "You guessed,
guessed, guessed
A, B, and C,
I see.
And now you get,
get, get
a grade of D!"

I Don't Want to Do Homework!

(To the tune of "Take Me Out to the Ball Game")

I don't want to do homework!
Please, I'm fed up with math!
Don't give assignments I'll surely botch.
Let me relax, I've got TV to watch!
And don't make me study my English.
I've learnt it real extra good!
So please say, "No homework tonight!"
'cause you know you should.

I don't want to do homework!
I don't want to plan maps!
Every day it is the same parade.
Think of the papers you won't have to grade!
So let's hear, "There'll be no more homework.
Go home and play with your friends!"
Though I know that's only a dream
until college ends!

I Got a Hall Pass

(To the tune of "Home on the Range")

I got a hall pass,
which means freedom from class.
Twice around the whole hallway I've strolled.
Five or six times, I think
I stopped to get a drink
and checked out where the fountains are cold!

Back to class and then
from that water I soon got a yen.
I had so quenched my thirst,
that I just had to burst!
And I needed a hall pass again!

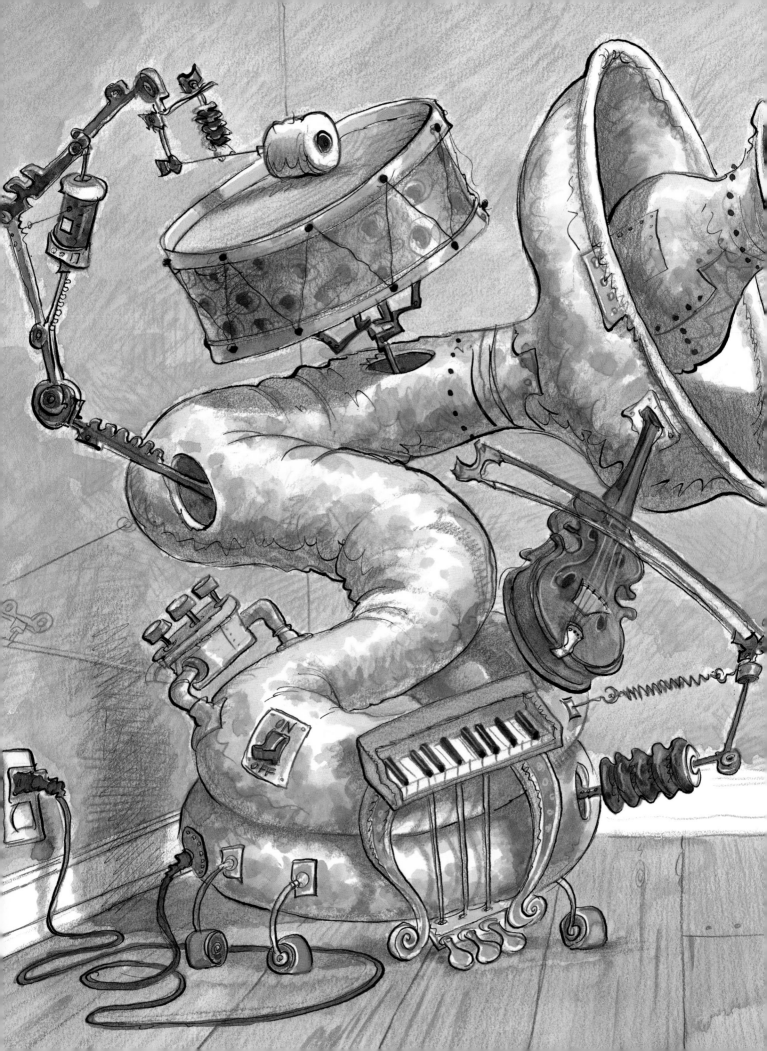

I Just Can't Play That Thing!

(To the tune of "The Battle Hymn of the Republic")

My teacher brings in instruments and says it's time to play.
I grab a violin and close my eyes and start to pray.
I screech the bow, and dogs and cats all howl and run away.
I just can't play that thing!

When it comes to making music,
I do not know what to do-sic!
Every note is just bad news-ic!
The teacher tried again!

She next gave me a tuba, then a piccolo and fife.
I blew till I turned blue but couldn't play them for my life.
The notes are A through G, but I hit P and caused her strife.
I just can't play those things!

When it comes to orchestration,
it's a no-win situation.
Teacher's new recommendation
is I am banned from band!

Tomorrow Is Our Class Picture Day!

(To the tune of "When Johnny Comes Marching Home")

Tomorrow is our class picture day!
Say cheese!
Say cheese!

The cameras'll be snapping away!
So please
don't sneeze!

Remember that face that you made last year?
And the thing that you stuck into Bobby's ear?
Don't do that again!
'Cause that picture got thrown away!

Tomorrow is our class picture day!
Behave!
Behave!

And don't come dressed like you live inside
a damp,
dark cave!

Don't wiggle or giggle and ruin the shot!
Tomorrow's the only chance we've got.
You're the principal—
be nice when it's picture day!

I Am in the Lunchroom!

(To the tune of "I'm a Little Teapot")

I am in the lunchroom!
Boy, I'm starved!
Wonder what kind of
food they've carved.
Chicken, fish, or meat loaf?
Maybe pork?
It's so hard, it snapped my fork!

I am in the lunchroom!
Salad's tossed!
Five mice from science
class just crossed!
Dancing in the dressing!
That's not right!
I just lost my appetite!

I am in the lunchroom!
Shoofly pie!
Made with fake shoo
and real fly!
If you get some, here's a
handy tip:
on your lap a no-pest strip!

I eat in this lunchroom
every day!
Why don't I bring lunch?
Well, no way!
It would not be better.
Poor, poor me!
My mom's the school lunch lady!

Lost and Found

(To the tune of "London Bridge Is Falling Down")

Lost and Found is full of me!
Golly gee!
There's my key!
And that looks like my left knee!
Glad I found it!

Lost and Found is full of I!
My, oh my!
There's my tie!
My notebook and my right eye!
Glad I found it!

One thing now is very clear:
All I own
is right here!
If I want my stuff real near,
I should move in!

At Recess We Just Run
Round and Round!

(To the tune of "The Wheels on the Bus")

At recess we just run round and round!
The playground's
where I'm bound!
I fling off the rings and hit the ground!
Hip, hip, hooray!

At recess we always throw the ball
at the wall
or at Paul!
The teacher says she can't take it all!
She's turning gray!

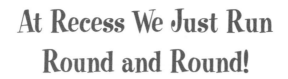

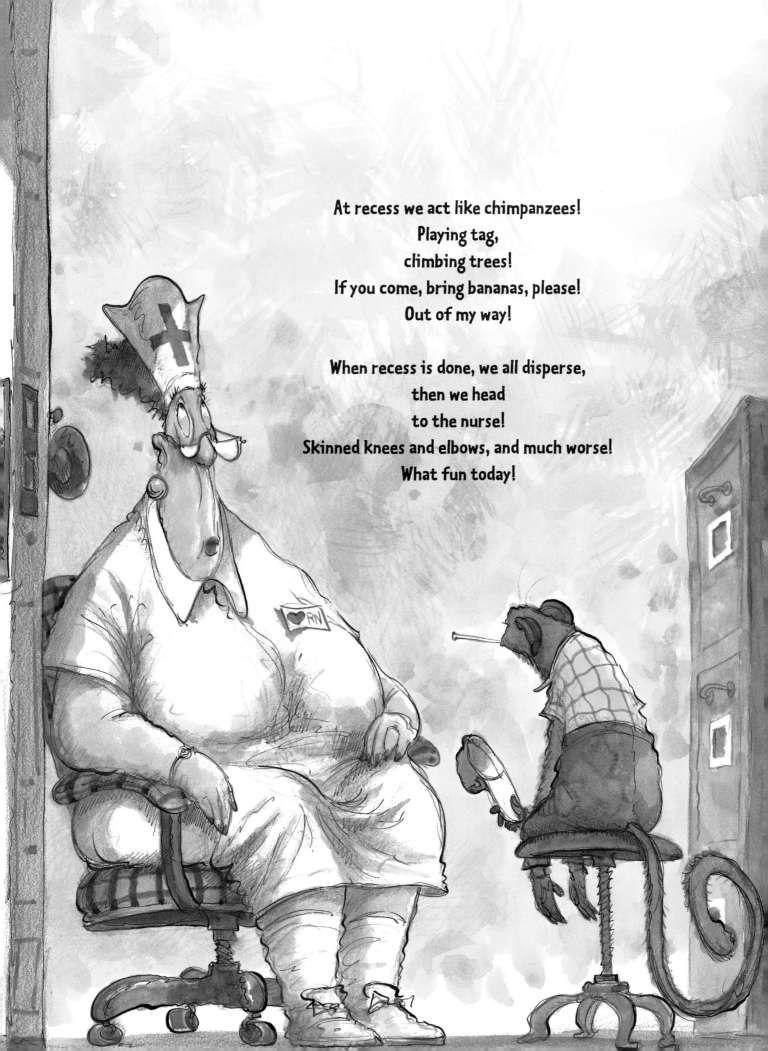

At recess we act like chimpanzees!
Playing tag,
climbing trees!
If you come, bring bananas, please!
Out of my way!

When recess is done, we all disperse,
then we head
to the nurse!
Skinned knees and elbows, and much worse!
What fun today!

Mad About Math

(To the tune of "Itsy Bitsy Spider")

Time for mul-ti-pli-ca-tion!
Like two times three times three.
The teacher knows the answer,
so why's she asking me?
This stuff is so confusing.
She says it is eighteen.
But I thought that that was two times nine,
so what does this all mean?

We're doing some division.
More math that I can't bear.
The problem is about a pie
four people need to share.
She says each gets a quarter.
I wish that she would cease.
Why do I care about a pie
if I don't get a piece?

Right now I'm staying after class.
It is 3:23.
The teacher says that we'll be here
till math makes sense to me.
I figured out there's thirty-seven minutes left till four,
and the teacher was so proud, she let me go
(I held the door).

It seems that I am good at math
when it's the only way.
Like figuring how long till lunch
and how long I can play.
So teachers, if you're listening,
I think you oughta try
to make math about things we like—
and don't forget the pie!

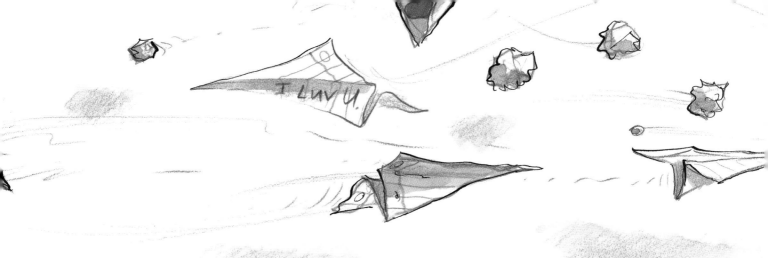

Passing Notes

(To the tune of "The Alphabet Song")

I just passed a note to Fred
and he handed it to Ned.
It contained
important text.
Sue and Al
got it next.
It was on its way to Chuck . . .
then—oh, no!—
disaster struck!

Teacher said,
"Is that for me?
Hand it over,
let me see!"
"No," I shrieked.
"Goodness' sake!
It's about your
birthday cake!
That is not meant for your eyes.
You will spoil the surprise!"

I thought I had gotten by,
but that was a foolish lie.
Her birthday
isn't soon.
It's in March—
this is June.
I learned passing notes is bad.
She passed one to Mom and Dad!

Oral Report Time

(To the tune of "Hey Diddle Diddle")

Oral report time!
I'm gonna get caught, I'm
just not prepared to present.
Did not do much thinkin'
'bout that old Abe Lincoln.
(He mighta been a president!)

Oral report time!
My speech'll be short, I'm
about to look dumb and weird.
Hey, this isn't funny.
I think he's on money.
(He might be the dude with the beard!)

Oral report time!
The kids'll all snort, I'm
in really kind of a mess.
Abe Lincoln, who is it?
(Perhaps I could visit
his famous Gettysburg Address.)

Oral report time!
Could use some support; I'm
about to do something wrong.
"Laryngitis I've got!"
I'll croak. "Teacher, I'll not
give the speech
and can't finish this song!"

FIG TREE

School Vacation

(To the tune of "Oh My Darling, Clementine")

School vacation!
What elation!
In just three short days we're done!
Then we're gonna
have some good times!
No more work, just full-time fun!

School vacation!
Celebration!
In just one day, oh how great!
Then we're gonna
have a party.
Park that bus, I'm sleeping late!

School vacation!
What frustration!
All my friends have gone away!
This is boring,
and I wish that
school could start again today!

School's in session!
What depression!
Now we're back, the time just flew!
Looking forward to vacation
is the thing that
gets me through!